A House with Bad Bones

Poetry by Adeline Tatum

QUILLKEEPERS PRESS

ISBN: 979-8-9891531-8-3

Published by Quillkeepers Press, LLC
PO Box 10236
Casa Grande, AZ 85130

through the wailing & the heaving

this heart of mine

softly whispers

get your pen and write

DEDICATION

Mother— I know you're now in a place large enough to house your heart. I love you and miss you every day. To my dear sister, Gildrette, I simply could not be here without you. You are truly the definition of unconditional love. Special thanks to Kristy Johnson, a friend, a mentor. Thank you for all your help and support and for helping me find my voice and place in poetry. To Mimi, Lily and Kiki,

I love you more than you know.

The House

Lives in Me

I was born in a house with bad bones.
I was seven when I saw him
push her through the door,
breaking her arm
in a cocaine-fueled rage.
I was dismantled
at a young age.
He was never really around, you know
he's gotta be a man.
He had gone out to get himself a brand-new life
with no room
for me or his past.
She wasn't ready for the flood
that would hit our home,
drowning herself in bottles of rum.
Perhaps nostalgia had begun spilling secrets
of the angry war vet
she could never please as a little girl.
I just don't know.
I don't think I can blame her, though.
Maybe she didn't know any better.
But in the end, it was these two,
who gave me life; who sealed my fate.
Who made me think love
feels like a punch in the face.
Begging and going after people who just don't care.
It was they, who left me to wonder
if I was invisible.
A deprived little girl with self-esteem issues.
Was it worth it?
I know when you die, you'll finally know
who I am.
I know you'll swim in a sea of my tears.
Maybe then you'll know I was real.

—Home

he stumbled into my room

after a drunken night

my prepubescent thighs

seemed like the right place

for his hands to dance

his rough fingers

run through

my soft curls

his black eyes

stare at me

with the hunger

of a thousand wolves

i was a snack

one for the taking

not quite ripe nor ready

starved eyes

peeping through

the window

find the glistening

bare skin

of unsuspecting

school girls

who shed

uniforms

on a warm and humid day

from a tender age

we were to accept

our bodies

did not belong to us

they are for the uninvited

to indulge

—boys will be boys

Summoned to consciousness

by grunts & moans.

A pair of wet lips

make their way down sacred places,

fingers swiftly ensue,

his carnivorous frenzy.

I remain still

like a photograph,

an illusion of a living thing

emanating no sound

but the sound my skin makes

as it crawls into my throat.

I keep my eyes tightly shut

in hopes oblivion

will swallow me whole

and I would somehow leave me

laying there in the dark.

—In the Dark

after endlessly

spinning in my head

the truth finally oozed

out of my cracked lips

she held my hand

in hers and said

me too

On a Friday night

she sat me down

and told me who he was

what he did to her

i could feel the confusion

she seemed like a little girl

standing there

while he took what he wanted

she was me & i was her

she sips on her beer & sounds almost proud

when she says, *my daddy nearly beat that man dead.*

—Mother

I remember what it felt like

to be nine years old and told

there must be something

wrong with me.

It was as if I had been fed

a spoonful of stupor,

turned into a speck

in a fragment of a second.

What I imagine trees feel

when they are ripped from the soil,

severed and turned into insignificant things.

Laying on my back,

on my grandmother's floor,

a ceiling fan is the only thing my eyes fixate on.

By this point, word had got out

of what happened that night.

It seemed the consensus was I must be crazy.

My grandmother hands me the house phone

and the voice on the other end says,

You need help, only someone who is mentally ill

would make this up

—Severed

On warm Saturday mornings,
we'd get in the car and crank the radio up,
make our way to the nearest beach.
It was my parents' favorite pastime.
We'd eat our meals under the sun,
I always found the salty air refreshing.
The waves come and go to wash
the bad things away, she used to say,
while the foamy water along the shoreline
drowned her red painted toenails.
For a moment, it felt just like she said,
as if it somehow could cleanse the ill
and we could be happy.

—The Beach

She sat in a dark room,
her favorite drink in hand—
Rum & Coke.
A 1980's TV set was the only light,
occasionally illuminating black mascara
mixed with damp, lifeless dreams,
streaming down her cheeks.

In the bedroom,
time is being abolished
with every shirt pulled
from hangers in the closet.
He hastily shoves a whole life
into a duffle bag and disappears
into the night.

And I am no comfort, you see,
as I naively touch her hand.
All I'm met with is a blank stare
that lasts for what feels like a lifetime.
She gulps her drink down again and again.

—Time

Life trickled through fingers,
like dirty water.
Familiar reflections of a life
lingered with a somber echo
so much sprouting inside,
but none of it could root her heart.

She tried to tame the wild animal
that left her old and withered,
as she watched the girl she wished to be
take the back seat.

Dead dreams festered and stunk
like rotten meat.
The stench chased her
through the streets
and she would disappear
into that good night
where there was no shortage of liquor
poured to drown demons.

She drank through every bottle
searching for him (or Jesus)
at the bottom.
Hoping she'd find him there
and be set free.

—Bottles

i try to sympathize with him

i think about how he might have been built

how generations of unfledged men sire

a pernicious bottomless pit

of deprivation & shame

of fathers who didn't know

how to hold their daughter's hands

    i still look for him in every man

—father

A House with Bad Bones

I'm standing on the sidewalk
looking for some [thing], perhaps,
some light.
A car door opens to my right,
a man in a tan suit gets out and says,
I think I'm supposed to pick you up.

His voice was as familiar as loneliness.
There was something about the way he carried himself,
the amber glasses he wore, the way he spoke.

The car ride was short
but filled with shy glances and small talk—
the weather,
how glad we were it was finally warming up,
after the winter,
a compliment through a gentle chuckle,
on how many colors I wore.

His sincere eyes,
he smelled like jasmine and cedarwood,
reminded me of the home I once had.

We arrived at our destination,
knowing the fall would be inevitable.
After the service & finding god,
he asked for my number, and I obliged.

—A Spring Day

his words flowed gently
like milk & honey
into my starved soul
into my rusted heart,
fatigued & mystified
my very own knight
scooping me up
from a pagan world
from dancing
under the city lights

a cold ring on my finger

the cord of three strands

youth's daisy chains

wrapped around my legs

When I look at him, I think—
could I crack his skull,
so, his thoughts would spill out?

I would

s

  c

    o

      u

        t

for secrets buried
in tiny boxes,
coated in shame,
hidden in darkness
for the sake of argument.

How does he feel? [What is he really thinking?]
Every night, we dine with misery.
A glass of wine tricks the mind into complacency.

I muster a smile,
as the sunrise
forces a new day upon me.

The house, the picket fence [domestic bliss]

peel my skin as I yield, gasping for air
and hide my true nature somewhere in the attic
collecting dust.

Animosity grows
like mold on these walls
and we've grown blind
to the stench.

Anger smeared words,
thrown like daggers,
give way to a shaky ground
and depravity emerges from the rubble.

I suppose at some point
we did love one another,

in
  our
    own
      deranged
        way.

My dear husband,
what have we done to each other?

—Marriage

every once in a while
i put him in my mouth
to keep the monster
from coming out

I like to lay on my side,

facing the window,

so the light that seeps

through the blinds

can paint my tears in crimson.

I'm wearing his handprints

around my neck again tonight.

He is really good at saying sorry.

And yet all he does is stitch my wounds

by sewing blame through them.

His words cut me with razor sharp regret

and I take the blame again like a nightcap,

finding solace in befriending silence.

—Necklace

A Stolen Voice

i still remember the silence

it was the only noise in my head

when you dragged me by my hair

& washed away all the evidence

in the river

& i cease to exist

vanished

into thin air

you took guilt out on a date

& buried it in the ground

so you could lay your head down

while i rot away

—murder

if the good book says

i am a body without a head

may i still speak?

will the words carved on my bones

fall on deaf ears?

they run the world & we have to adhere

offer our bodies as temples

for them to feast on blood & tears

& live out our years unable to speak

—the bible

for as long as i can remember

my heart yearned to belong somewhere

i had found solace within the walls of his structure

& the promise of a purposeful life.

they sang songs about a dead-less death

& building mansions in paradise

there amongst my tribe

i was being washed of dirt & sins

emerging clean from the waters of baptism

a rebirth

how was i to know

the secrets they kept

would bury me alive?

—take me to church

the bible says

a crime should be witnessed by two

[or it didn't happen]

it is not in the voice of youth

who tremble in their innocence

what do you know about life, little girl?

she points to her doll

to show where she was touched

but no one was around?

does god cover his eyes

when little girls are being hurt?

—the two witness rule

What does it mean to be *God-fearing* men?

Girls, wear your Sunday best
and sit next to your brothers in faith,
who sweep transgressions under the rug
while singing about forgiveness.

God is merciful- oh yes!

He also looks the other way
and gives you a prescription to pray,
ten times a day,
when you've given into sin,
no matter how horrendous,

...it's just another Sunday.

—Good Men

you've made me small & shapeless

left me lurking around death's door

starved for a crown—i've eaten every vile word

from your tongue as we stand on this tainted slate

redemption calls like the raven

but i'm not sure i'll ever make it

passed the skeletons & a stone that reads

'here she lies buried alive'

—smothered

I try not to think of you.

After all, it happened so long ago,

but it seems like not even time can fix you

nor fade your sins away.

You sit there all too pleasantly

in your flimsy house of cards;

while I'm hunched over my bed of bones,

seeking atonement from ghosts

in a nightmare I forgot to wake up from.

You took my mouth for your own and snuffed my pain

because you were too afraid of what it might say.

You left me on bleeding knees and fed me to a beast

all too familiar.

I escape,

perhaps through your raptured chest.

And I will never come back until

you whisper your regrets into my skin,

and bind me with recompense

before you deem me godless.

—House of Cards

We haven't talked in a while. I'm not sure you've noticed
but I've been a little preoccupied licking my wounds,
to salvage any ounce of empathy I have left
and not set this house ablaze.

The truth is the anger has seeped through and
stained my bones. It has crippled me and
made me cold, made it hard to walk the path you lit for me
all those years ago.

To be honest, I'm not sure I believe it anymore.
I will not stand by them, those who make a spectacle
of singing your name while turning a blind eye
to the pain and suffering they've caused.

And where were you, if I may ask?
When the walls were inching closer and
closer, leaving me in a suffocating panic
with nowhere to turn but a world of darkness.
Where are you now? My wounds are screaming loud and
I'm searching for the path through these molten rocks.
Hey God, I am trying. I hope that is enough.

—A Letter to God

Is it here, in this place,

where I will find peace?

Is it here amongst the trees,

surrounded by efflorescence,

as flowers strew their cool

odors in a blanket of wind,

cradling me to sleep?

Is this where I will

find what they call

God, the source of

all things?

Will it restore me,

restore this life?

Where I will finally

lay down, and the sky

and I can have an open

conversation, and I will be cured?

Searching for

the Compass

I spend most nights on the edge,

trying to decipher the secret code

carved on my skin.

At times, I can smell her, that familiar

scent of her embrace, as a kid.

I wonder if she shaped me, in some ways,

with the jagged parts of herself she hid.

Am I another ship adrift, aimlessly

floating, never to reach shore?

Or will I seize the helm and steer

my own boat through the storm?

I waiver between us two.

Am I as empty vessel as she was, at times?

Most nights, I decide—

I am the compass.

—The Compass

Truth serum courses through my veins.
An intruder broke in and injected it
into my skin. How else could I explain
how today, as the sun rose,
I wasn't compelled to lie anymore?
My lungs ache, they're corrupted
from breathing the air of a selfish world.
Why should I get out of bed every morning,
wearing the cloak of contentment?
I'm broken and don't know what
can put me together.
I wonder, was I ever whole?
This life seems like a place
where my hopes and dreams meet.
Yet, their demise
chewed me up
and spat me back out.

the road to the promised land is not linear
[or so they say]. yet, it undulates
with past heartaches as backdrops
and whispers of ancient catastrophes
that seep through like relics.
i think i may have done all this resurrecting
for nothing
i am ever so

s
  l
    a
      n
       t
        e
         d

in self-loathing monologues.
eager to pounce on my neck
while in line at the coffee shop
[is this healing?]
crawling on bare knees
along this skewed path,
lost in days
where frail constitutions
fail to be fruitful.
when the pain is gone,
will I even like myself anymore?
i am a daughter of darkness,
who now and then
lies to herself and declares
she can catch a glimpse of it.
but, if this is healing,
then i think i'd rather be dead.

it's not too late [they say].
am i there, yet?

—healing

They say images of an entire life

will flood the mind when one dies.

But all I saw was her jaw dropping,

her chest heaving for air,

and the breath escaping her.

Flashes of her dancing to Spanish songs,

as I hid under the coffee table

to watch her float across the floor like an angel.

An echoing voice saying, *you have cancer.*

A gray hand sticking out of the sand.

The L-shaped crack staring back at me

from the ceiling on nights

sleep would simply evade me.

Perhaps I, too, know what it's like to die,

for this mattress feels more like my coffin.

—Insomnia

I wish I could say
that I took to silence to digest
the unsaid.
But there was no pause
nor any *'aha'* moments
while crying in cars.

That is to say,
I'm still afraid of the dark.
I can still hear the ghosts
who have been buried by the rush
to live and devour the world.
Whose faint but sorrowful cries
keep me company
on insomniac nights.

That is to say,
I still haven't found me,
despite relentlessly searching
in empty cabinets
and in between moments
when you still loved me.

The Search

for Love

my first kiss
birthed the infectious idea
that love could save me

A House with Bad Bones

Perhaps that day can best
be described as fate.
Him—sitting in front of me,
black jeans, black tee.

Amber-colored hair hidden
under a worn out hat.
He said things I imagine
a God would say—like
everything happens for a reason,
even if you don't see it right away.

I wanted, so very badly, to be
that cup of coffee he savored
with slow snacking lips.
I wanted to reach out for him,
cup my hands—to make a place
for him to sleep.

I wanted to be smeared across
his eyelids so he would see me,
—always.

How could we have known
we were on a collision course?
One that would last long after
our cups—ran dry.

—Coffee Date

this place

a fool's paradise

i watch my dreams

drift away with swirling

seas

that carry our fragmented

story

this sticky honey heat

makes it hard to breathe

under orange

skies

when the sun

sets

i dance with lost love's lament

—miami

A sense of foreboding

creeps up my chest.

Did he hear my heart stop?

I tried to keep a straight face,

when he stood up to undo his belt.

The lights were blinding me,

as if I was staring into the sun.

He looked like some kind of god,

glowing before me.

I hear the clicking sound his camera made,

when he captured me in my nightgown.

I get down on my knees.

I would have let him drag me around like an animal,

if it meant he would not leave.

Click [he takes another picture].

Open your mouth [he whispers].

Click, click,

you're so good at this.

—The Photographer

his lips are sweet & dark

like red wine

his voice rattles the sky

he walks over to me

& asks me for a dance

said he would keep me safe

is this a memory

or a mirage...

i blink & he begins to dissolve

faded into the night

like a poem i'm meant to write

take me like a vitamin

into the depths

of your bones

& i will find a spot

to lay my head on

where i will

breathe in your

dreams & tame

the nightmares

that keep you awake

let me live there

amongst the chaos

of your thoughts

whispering soft

i love you's

for years to come

The dark has its way

of levying desperation,

pushing me into a state of emergency.

Sitting on my front porch

exhausted and cold.

The night comes crawling,

the moon glares with wishful remorse

of an old lover

exposing my hunger.

The bare branches of a silver birch tremble.

We are both shaken on this blustery night.

Every ounce of me whispers, then shouts

your name in unison.

I inhale every discarded kiss and overdose

on your lips under the moonlight.

i once told you

i would leave you alone

but you haven't left me.

i still carry your secrets in my skin.

you stormed my body like a riot

& to be honest i'm not sure how

to leave it all behind

how to live and breathe

in this swamp with no silver lining

in the aftermath of our catastrophe

The truth I hide from most

that I've been hounding this

feeling through the mud,

diluting myself into a

sweet elixir you can gulp.

It was never you; it was never us.

And if I'm being

honest, I liked the feeling

of falling a little too much.

I bear the marks of that monster

on me. A bitter love affair.

One that left me sobbing

on an old mattress in the street.

With bated breath,

wishing the filthy

sorrow away

until it no longer aches

until my lungs have inhaled

it all gone and my blue moon

turns to gold again.

this cursed existence

watching you burn ever bright

a you without i

i've swallowed your lies

like i swallowed you

quietly in the dark.

he smells my decay

& hovers around

like a vulture

in the sky

he has me on my knees

sucking him for his eye

while he tells a story

about how he can't love anyone

[since you left]

life is a big waiting room

full of vintage whispers

echoing on the walls

i dust all the remnants of us

off the surface

and open the curtains

to let in the rays of hope

because i've been trying

my hardest to make it home

How quickly can this place be

stripped of its color?

And I of hopeful breath?

Walking in circles

in an empty lot, as you explain

you were going back home.

Now, my nights consist of

laying out maps to count

the space in finger-length

between where you are and where I lay.

Cutting holes in the ceiling,

so I can stare at cardboard-cutout stars

wishing you were somewhere out there,

staring back.

How many times must we say goodbye?

A House with Bad Bones

I'd like to say

I've laid your ghost to rest.

Buried it underneath many cycles

of the moon, overthrown

by the sun.

Stifled beneath countless 'x' marks

on calendar days

I no longer remember

hazelnut freckles on your face

or your heart shaped lips.

In truth, the past is not over

it is a bottomless pit,

where the undead gather to feast

unforgivingly on my sanity.

It haunts me still

like ghostly lights

in the rearview mirror

on country roads.

O, the past,

the past is not done with us.

I tucked you away

and braced myself

for the waves

that would slowly erode us.

We've been dancing

on the edge of forgiveness ever since,

somehow eluding it.

When I am ripe,

would you take my hand

or would you stash me away

in places no longer worth consuming?

I am lost in the abundance of your hurt

no longer human

but something worse.

Spending my days

sniffing old pages

and translating you

over and over again.

Time smells of your embrace

and the eagerness of my younger days.

In my dreams,

you quit wearing

keychains on your black jeans.

You grow your hair out

and play the guitar.

You're no longer preoccupied

with chasing butterflies

in the meadows.

You tell me that life is a birdsong

and that I was the mountain

you couldn't lay your head on

at night—to say your prayers

and hope life didn't feel like you've settled

or as if you couldn't take a breather.

but the mornings always find me the same way

feeling as if

I haven't inhaled in years.

what if i roar

like the storms

that roll across the east coast

will i then be sired in him?

these nights—once young & peaceful

become old & weathered

manning isolation

i writhe on the soil

till my hair becomes matted

for i know what it's like to

hold my breath

to be a speck

a notion waiting to inhale

so i plead

a hymn for beauty

so she may remember me

here i am

where you left me

in the gray—the space

between hope and letting go

it's where you'll find me

turning tears into words

bleeding onto paper

for warmth

A House with Bad Bones

At dusk,

when hues of gold & tangerine

swallow the sunset & the wind rattles

between the leaves, coupling the birds

singing their songs.

All is seemingly unaware & unbothered by your absence.

But I am reminded of it,

how your name bears

the sudden burst of life

that sits at the edge of spring,

the loud rumbling of a thunderstorm

on a summer evening

& the cool scent of wisteria

& night blooming jasmine.

On nights like these, I am reminded

of the ink smear on my skin

from discarded poems

you left in your wake.

You're still the life in my lungs

& the taste of despair in my coffee every morning, even after the illusion of time

inches by my window.

Time is no match for you

& if I had one wish,

before death gifts me wings,

it would be to undress this night

with your head resting on my chest.

Hope of

Healing

My mother used to utter the words,
Dios hizo un dia detras del otro.
Which means *God made one day after another.*
Those words now echo in my head
like ripples on a lake.
I reckon it means we all get second chances.
It's funny how she was kind of optimistic
in that way. Lately, it's been mighty hard to see,
unsure of what I ought to be.

Time is heavy on me,
tedious even.
I ponder all the things I could have been
if I had used it wisely.
I long to prove my worth on this earth
& to become something.
So, I pray.
I pray the days are forgiving
of my misuse of them.
I pray the sun rises on this sleeping songbird
& it wakes to find his voice again.
I pray the ink won't run out,
before I've penned all I need to say.

i'm not afraid of those lovely dark deep woods

nor will i say i do not hear them call my name

in the night.

if i ran to them

& pressed my ear against the ground

i'd hear the sound of my sisters singing

through the ache

i would let my tears cleanse

the carcass that remains

& chant until she opens her mouth

to let us in.

i think i've replaced

you with pen & paper.

words are flowing out

like endless rain into a paper cup

writing memories away

& into archives

of my mind

every day i find

myself thinking

a little less of you

& a little more of me

a new love

i will let you be free

swimming through clouds

where the fog lies kissing the mountainside

for that is where you wish to be

enamored with skies that kiss you

with the winds of freedom

& let your heart be unfettered, true to life

but hope will not perish

for it is timeless like a sundial in the night

& if you ever call

i'll run to be by your side

i want to be at peace

but; i am the push & pull

of being alive

living between lines & daydreams

where should i run

when they say my reflection is my truth?

i have loved at all costs & shattered at loss

but; i am still alive

savoring the sweet & tart flavors of life

my eyes still marvel at cotton candy skies

& the wet grass underneath my feet

i will float on like the summer breeze

& live;

till he says he has room for me

perhaps hope is not
the thing with feathers
somehow evading me

perhaps it exists
in the expanding
of my lungs
when i tell myself
to breathe

perhaps it lives
in the hiatus
from the yearning
of my sinews
to cry out his name

perhaps it's in the way
i now turn the page
to find seasons
stretched across
his remnants

Mom said I was like her
wanted to swallow the world whole,
while i sat on the sidewalk
paralyzed and doused in fear,
unable to run after it all.

I've been dreaming my life away,
instead of paying heed
to the ones who came before me.
The musicians & visionaries
who chased after siren songs
quenching their thirst for life.

Will I ever make it?
Will I live to be older than she was?
Sister, will you hold my hand?
Brother, will you be alright?
[Mom, watch over Dad]
Gil, stop worrying so much.
Our tree grows strong
& the kids will be fine
I've been dreaming my whole life,
only this time, I'm waking up.

—Family Tree

Adeline is a poet who grew up in a small town in IL. She attended Kankakee Community College, pursuing a degree in Psychology, and is currently studying Creative Writing. She was first published in the 2022 winter issue of the literary magazine *Sequoia Speaks*. She since has been featured in several poetry anthologies including, *Because I F*cking Said So*, *Harvest*, and *Sapling*.